The History of

Mail

Data

Dona Herweck Rice

Consultants

Colene Van Brunt
Math Coach
Hillsborough County Public Schools

Publishing Credits

Rachelle Cracchiolo, M.S.Ed., *Publisher*
Conni Medina, M.A.Ed., *Managing Editor*
Dona Herweck Rice, *Series Developer*
Emily R. Smith, M.A.Ed., *Series Developer*
Diana Kenney, M.A.Ed., NBCT, *Content Director*
June Kikuchi, *Content Director*
Susan Daddis, M.A.Ed., *Editor*
Karen Malaska, M.Ed., *Editor*
Kevin Panter, *Senior Graphic Designer*

Image Credits: back cover irisphoto1/Shutterstock; pp.10–11 Look and Learn/ Bridgeman Images; pp.12–13 Interfoto/Alamy; p.14 (insert) Kiev Victor/Shutterstock; all other images from iStock and/or Shutterstock.

Library of Congress Cataloging-in-Publication Data

Names: Rice, Dona, author.
Title: The history of mail / Dona Herweck Rice.
Description: Huntington Beach, CA : Teacher Created Materials, [2019] | Includes index. |
Identifiers: LCCN 2017055023 (print) | LCCN 2017058099 (ebook) | ISBN 9781480759824 (eBook) | ISBN 9781425856885 (pbk.)
Subjects: LCSH: Postal service--History--Juvenile literature.
Classification: LCC HE6078 (ebook) | LCC HE6078 .R53 2019 (print) | DDC 383/.49--dc23
LC record available at https://lccn.loc.gov/2017055023

Teacher Created Materials
5301 Oceanus Drive
Huntington Beach, CA 92649-1030
www.tcmpub.com

ISBN 978-1-4258-5688-5

Table of Contents

Mail Call!

You open your **mailbox**. Mail is inside!

How did it get there?

About Mail

People have sent mail for a long time.

Most mail has been sent on paper.

POSTAGE PAID
POSTAGE PAID
Mr. P. Smith
Unit 1
22 Main Street
Metrocity
4002

Mail can be sent a short way. It can be sent a long way.

It can even be sent around the world!

Let's Do Math!

Scott, Clare, and Milo all check their mailboxes for letters. Compare the data. Use numbers to complete the sentences.

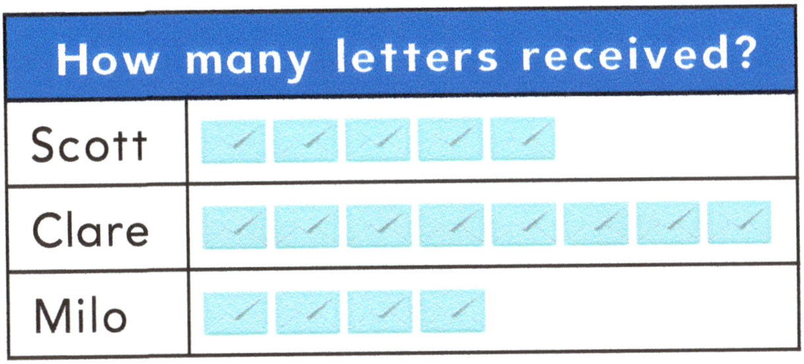

represents one letter.

1. Clare receives ______ more letters than Scott.

2. Milo receives ______ fewer letters than Clare.

3. Scott, Clare, and Milo receive ______ letters total.

The First Mail

Some of the first people to send mail were from China. They walked or rode horses to carry it.

This man rode
a long way to
deliver a letter.

The people of ancient Rome also had mail. They **often** carried it by horse and cart.

Let's Do Math!

Jada asks students in her class how their mail carriers deliver mail. Complete the sentences using *walk*, *bike*, or *drive*.

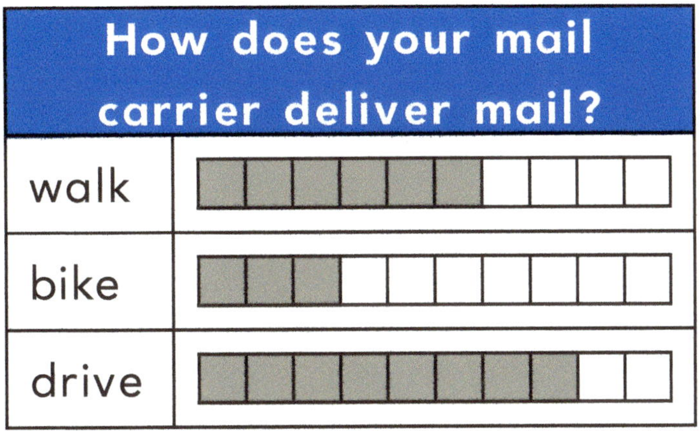

1. More mail carriers ______ than ______.

2. Fewer mail carriers ______ than ______.

3. Three more mail carriers ______ than ______.

The people of France had the first **post office**. People put stamps on mail. Many people could send and receive mail.

This post office is in France.

Let's Do Math!

Mrs. Hall's class votes on the stamp they like best. Use the table to answer the questions.

Which stamp do you like best?	
tree	Sadi, Pia, Ken, Milo, Burt, Kai
house	Ana, Joe, Tara, Sal
star	Das, Zina, Jada, Mika, Lee, Jack, Sid

1. How many students voted? How do you know?
2. How many more students like star stamps than tree stamps? How do you know?

Mail Today

People still send and receive mail. But mail is not **always** on paper.

Email
Mail
COMPOSE
All
More
Inbox (169)
Starred
Sent Mail
Drafts (10)
Notes
More
me,custormer (2) Re : company info ...
email (no subject) ...
me,friends (6) Re : 2 new notifica ...
custormer no.249 Re : company info ...
me,custormer (2) Re : company info ...
me,custormer Meeting today ...
Join us New Sign-in on Computer ...
me,custormer (1) Re : On 23 October at 09:00, ...
email What do you thimk so far? ...
custormer no.001 company info ...
custormer (no subject) ...
me,custormer we want some ...
me,custormer (2) Re : company info ...
email (no subject) ...

Mail today is often sent **online**. People use many types of **screens**.

There is no end to where and how mail can go!

Problem Solving

The ways people send and receive mail has changed over the years. One thing has not changed. People like getting mail from family and friends. Find out more by collecting and comparing data.

1. Draw a table like the one on page 21. Ask 15 people what type of mail they like. Write their names in the table.

2. Most people like ______. I know this because ______.

3. People like ______ least. I know this because ______.

4. Write a "How many more" question about the data.

What type of mail do you like?	
paper mail	
email	
class notes	

Glossary

always—all the time

mailbox—box where mail is delivered and picked up

often—much of the time

online—on the Internet

post office—a business where mail is received, sorted, and delivered

screens—the flat parts of computers, TVs, or other devices where images and words are shown

Index

Answer Key

Let's Do Math!

page 9:

1. 3
2. 4
3. 17

page 13:

Answers will vary for questions 1 and 2.

1. walk; bike
2. bike; drive
3. walk; bike

page 15:

1. 17; counting names
2. 1; counting students who liked each stamp and subtracting

Problem Solving

All answers will vary.